LIONS

Printed in Hong Kong

98 99 00 01 02 5 4 3 2 1

Library of Congress Cataloging-in-Publication Data
Bertram, Brian C.R., 1944–
Lions / by Brian Bertram.
p.   cm. — (World life library)
Includes index.
ISBN 0-89658-399-6
1. Lions. I. Title. II. Series.
QL737.C23B466 1998   98-17626
599.757–dc21   CIP

Distributed in Canada by Raincoast Books, 8680 Cambie Street, Vancouver, B.C. V6P 6M9

Published by Voyageur Press, Inc.
123 North Second Street, P. O. Box 338, Stillwater, MN 55082 U.S.A.
651-430-2210, fax 651-430-2211

Educators, fundraisers, premium and gift buyers, publicists and marketing managers:
Looking for creative products and new sales ideas? Voyageur Press books are available at special
discounts when purchased in quantities, and special editions can be created to your
specifications. For details contact the marketing department at 800-888-9653.

LIONS

Brian Bertram

Voyageur Press

LIONS

Brian Bertram

Voyageur Press

Contents

The Life of Lions

How the title the 'King of Beasts' was acquired is not clear, nor how well deserved it is. Nonetheless there are aspects of the life of lions that are distinctly like a monarch's — they command respect, and they have problems with family and with subjects.

Everybody knows roughly what a lion looks like — it is essentially a very large cat, with a strong but agile body, piercing eyes, immaculate fur, and sleepy nature. But lions are not just any cats. They are the second largest of the 35 species of cats, only just smaller than the largest races of tiger. They are unique among cats in that the two sexes look strikingly different: an adult male has a large mane of hair on his head and shoulders, which makes him look larger than he is, and much larger than a lioness. Like in the other large cats, the male is in fact 30-50 per cent bigger (i.e. heavier) than the female. His mane is darker than the rest of his coat, sometimes black, and helps to make the owner look not only more formidable but also conspicuous from hundreds of feet away. Less noticeable, and found in no other cats, is the black tuft of hair on the tip of the tail of grown lions of both sexes; it has no obvious function, other than as a toy for lion cubs to play with.

A lion has the tools it needs for its demanding role in its environment. It has large canine teeth that are crucial both for holding prey and for fighting other lions, and it has powerful shearing molar teeth adapted for cutting up animal tissue. As is typical of cats, the sharp hooked claws can be retracted into sheaths in the paws when not in use, so they remain sharp for when they are needed — to seize prey, to fight, and to climb. The eyes are large, and lions clearly have excellent eyesight. By day they can see distant happenings about as well as human beings can, but at night they can do much better than us,

A lioness seeks her supper.

thanks to a light-reflecting layer on the retina which enables very low amounts of light in effect to be used twice over. When you shine a torch at a lion at night you see its eyes reflecting big and bright before it quickly looks away.

Lions (males and females) are unique among the world's cats in being highly social animals. Usually, if you are lucky enough to encounter a tiger, puma, leopard, lynx or whatever, it is likely to be on its own. A lion on the other hand will generally be with companions. Lions live in social units called 'prides' which consist of long-lasting extended families. They are not together all the time, but will often split off into sub-groups or singletons and travel independently. Nevertheless they are all part of the same social unit, they occupy the same range, and they will meet one another every few hours or days, and will interact amicably with one another when they do. There can be up to about a dozen adult females in a pride, from one to six adult males, and a whole lot of cubs of various ages. The pride will sometimes be widely scattered in their range, sometimes all crowded together in the same small patch of shade, sometimes dispersed as they dash after panicking prey, and sometimes gathered again as a seething mass at a warm kill.

Much of what is known about the life of lions in the wild has come from long-term studies of them in the Serengeti National Park in Tanzania. Starting in 1966, George Schaller, then I, then David Bygott and Jeanette Hanby, and then Craig Packer and Anne Pusey, and several associates, have been able to keep tabs on the fortunes of individually recognized lions and their prides for over 30 years. There have been few other studies of individual wild animals that have been going so long, or that have yielded so much information.

Studying wild lions needs a lot of patience, because most of the time very little is going on. Our field work in East Africa revealed that lions spend almost 80 per cent of their time inactive, either sleeping, lying or sitting doing nothing.

A sleeping male's face, with scars that help make him recognizable.

Like all cats, lions drink by lapping.
If necessary, but not by choice, they can go for days without water.

They spend 10-15 per cent of their time travelling, covering about 3-5½ miles (5-9 km) a day, having to move a bit more when or where food is in short supply. On average they spend 5-8 per cent of their time actively hunting prey and (if successful) eating it. They spend 1-2 per cent of their time on social interactions with one another. Most activity takes place at night, but they do a lot of resting then too; equally, they are ready to rush into action by day, particularly before and after the hottest periods, should interesting situations arise. But usually they don't.

Lions clearly know the geography of their range. They know the watering points where they can go to drink after feeding; they know the likely places where gazelles might be ambushed coming down to drink; they know where are the secluded rock crevices where their small cubs can be safely left; and they know where are the most comfortable resting places, on cool moist sandbanks beside empty stream beds, under spreading shady acacia trees, on the rounded granite kopjes (rock outcrops) that litter the Serengeti, and in a few places on broad horizontal tree branches in the breeze and up out of the way of elephants, biting flies or tourist vehicles.

There is no breeding season for lions, and cubs may be conceived or born at any time of the year, wet season or dry. A young lioness comes into estrus first when she is between three and four years old. An estrous female is easily recognizable: she tends to be lying conspicuously out in the open, apparently less conscious of the heat, and has a male close beside her, following her wherever she goes, which is not far. After a bit she rises, maybe solicits the male's attention by head-rubbing and trotting past him, and then crouches. Mating is rapid, with the male almost biting the skin of the lioness' neck, and then dismounting quickly as the female turns with a snarl and perhaps a swat before flopping onto her side or back again. The pair repeats the performance again and again, every 10-15 minutes for usually between two and five days. Nonetheless, despite all this effort, she is not likely to produce cubs as a result, but comes back into estrus again a few weeks later. On average, only about one in five mating periods results in the birth of a litter of cubs.

If she does become pregnant, her pregnancy is surprisingly short for so large an animal — only three-and-a-half months. Newborn cubs are very small (less than 1 per cent of their mother's weight) and their eyes are closed. In almost all litters there are up to four cubs, usually two or three; however, it is virtually impossible to know numbers because they are kept concealed for the first few weeks of life. Their mother sometimes moves their hiding place, and I occasionally came across a lioness carrying carefully in her huge mouth a tiny cub that she was transferring from one thicket or rock crevice to another.

After four to six weeks the cubs are able to walk well enough to follow their mother, who leads the faintly spotted little creatures out to meet others of the pride. They join up with other cubs and generally travel around together and with their mother for the next couple of years. The adults go off hunting, and then return to guard and suckle their cubs, or to lead them to a prey animal they have managed to catch. The cubs take only milk for about their first three months, then start to eat meat as well, and are finally weaned off milk between six and eight months old.

Cubs, like adults, spend a lot of time inactive, although they play among one another unless food is in very short supply. They grow quite fast if food is reasonably abundant and after about four months follow the adults everywhere. They follow behind on hunts, and seem to be taking in the skills that they are going to need in the future. By a year old, the males among them have become recognizable, both from their rear ends and from the sparse longer hairs that will gradually develop into the adult male's fine mane.

The turning point in the life of young lions is two-and-a-half to three years. At that stage they are nearly full-sized but not as bulky as mature animals. Most young females stay on in their pride and become breeding lionesses there. However, if the pride has been doing particularly well and is

In the course of their travels with the pride,
cubs learn all the features of their group territory.

in effect full of females, some of the adolescent females will leave their pride's range at that age and start to wander, apparently looking for an unoccupied place where they can settle and where there will be food all year round. Such places are scarce and hard to find, for most are already occupied by lions. Therefore most departing females will lead a fairly unsuccessful nomadic life.

By contrast, all the young males have to leave the pride of their birth at the end of their adolescence. They go as a group, with any other young male companions with whom they have grown up. They wander nomadically, going wherever food can be found. In the Serengeti, that means following the huge migrating herds of mooing wildebeest and braying zebras which follow the seasonal rains out onto the open grass plains and then retreat into the western and northern woodlands in the dry season. These young males travel around for a couple of years as they grow in knowledge, might and mane. They eventually manage to find and take over a pride of females and to become the breeding adult males there. For a few years they live a reproductively busy life. They retain tenure of their pride for a few years until, older and weaker and fewer, they are replaced by new males, and must become nomads again for the short remainder of their lives. A wild male's life is usually over after about 12 years, whereas a female with the support of her pride may well live to between 15 and 18 years.

An average lion generation time of about 10 years is a tiny fraction of the time that lions have been on this planet. Lions were spread through Europe, Asia, Africa and North America between 100,000 and 10,000 years ago. The common ancestor of the present-day large cats of the *Panthera* genus (lion, tiger, leopard, snow leopard, and jaguar) lived about 5 million years ago. And that was about 55 million years after the sudden disappearance of the large dinosaurs which for three times as long up until then had included the planet's dominant predators. Lions, like us, are relative newcomers.

An adult male can expect to have a 5-10 year reproductive life.

The Lion's Niche

In their huge range in Africa, lions occupy a wide variety of habitats. They may be found from sea level up to over 13,000 ft (4000 m) in altitude, looking incongruous in mountain mist, and from the bamboo forest there out to near-desert. Almost the only African habitats in which they are not found are in the parched interiors of deserts or the humid depths of tropical rain forests. The main thing they depend upon is an adequate prey base — sufficient large enough animals for them to feed upon and an environment in which they can catch them. Not surprisingly, in areas where prey are consistently more abundant, as in some of the East African national parks, lion population densities are able to be far higher than elsewhere, and can reach as many as 20 lions per 40 sq miles (100 sq km). By contrast, in arid areas of southern Africa, lions live at only about 10 per cent of that density.

A lion's life is not an easy one. For a start, as most people do not appreciate, catching their prey is extremely difficult for them. True, a lion is a superb athlete, able to sprint at perhaps 30-37 mph (50-60 kph). Nonetheless, most prey animals can sprint faster still, because they have more slender and lighter legs, and of course, they are adapted to avoid being caught by predators. Therefore the great problem for a lioness is how to get within such close range of unalerted prey that she can sprint and catch it before the prey has had time to dash away even faster.

I say 'she' because most hunting is done by the female lions, for two reasons. Partly, the male can wait idly by until the females have captured their meal, and then being bigger and stronger he is able to muscle in on their kill and get a disproportionate share (the lion's share) of the results of the lionesses' hard work. Partly, those lionesses are probably better at most kinds

Rock outcrops ('kopjes') provide fine vantage points for looking for prey.

of hunting, with their more slender agile form and without the conspicuous great mane on the male's head and shoulders.

A lioness is very skillful at stalking unseen towards her intended victim. She fixes her eyes on it, head high at first, nose and ears forward. She advances smoothly, using available bits of cover, freezing when the prey looks up, and creeping on again when it resumes feeding. It is a deadly game of 'Grandmother's Footsteps'. Her body seems to shrink sinuously below her as she advances. She is patient, and may wait many minutes or more if there is no concealed route along which to advance, or while allowing the prey to move unaware towards her. At some point, when she thinks she is close enough, she sprints out, and may be able to make sufficient contact with the fleeing prey to pull it down. If so, she rapidly seizes and suffocates it by clamping her teeth onto either the throat or the muzzle.

Fortunately, from the point of view of the potential meal, things usually do not turn out that way. Very often the object of her attentions drifts away out of range without ever being aware of her presence or of its own danger. Sometimes the intended prey catches her smell, and dashes off with a sharp snort or whistle of alarm. Sometimes the lioness charges but the prey sprints off faster, or dodges round an obstruction and escapes. The great majority of lion hunts fail: on fewer than 25 per cent of times when a lioness charges does she catch her prey, whereas on many other occasions she does not even manage to stalk close enough for a charge to be worthwhile.

Success in hunting is unpredictable. It is always on the cards that the fleeing prey may slip, or trip in a hole, or collide with another, or run the wrong way. Lionesses can improve their chances in several ways. Hunting at night, particularly on dark moonless nights, is generally more successful than by day, not surprisingly, because the dark provides concealment. By targeting individual prey animals that are particularly vulnerable – injured, sick, very young, slow, or isolated – lions can increase their chances of ending up with a meal.

A lioness stalking silently towards possible prey.
Her shoulder blades are the highest point of her body.

Top: A skirmish at a small carcass.
Bottom: Most lion hunts fail, especially with inexperienced young male hunters.

Choosing the right terrain for their efforts also helps, where escape routes may be limited. A wind generally seems to help them, probably because it drowns any sound of their approach, but in most places lions do not seem to be able to take in the importance of wind direction: they will often approach from upwind instead of from downwind, and so alert the prey.

All these are important factors, but the main way in which lions can improve their hunting chances is by hunting cooperatively. Several lionesses spread out, and stalk in different directions towards the prey. In at least some places individual lionesses specialize by tending to take up particular positions relative to one another – they specialize as centres or wingers, for example, and they do better when in their preferred hunting positions.

A great advantage of group hunting is that when a prey animal has detected a lioness it does not have a safe direction in which to flee: 'away' may simply mean passing near to another unseen lioness poised to charge. Contrary to some of the older stories, there is no good evidence that some lions in the group can openly drive prey towards other waiting hunters, but certainly the chaos of group hunts, with prey running in panic in different directions, results in much greater chances that prey will be caught. Quite often in these group hunts, more than one prey animal will fall victim, caught independently by different lionesses, and then there is even more food for the pride to feed on.

Lions are great opportunists, and will readily exploit other situations that arise unexpectedly. Many a time I have seen a clearly non-hunting, inactive, resting lioness slink into action on seeing, for example, a group of zebras approaching a watering point where she might be able to ambush them. Lions in the Serengeti are particularly quick to spot and ambush the migrating long lines of galloping wildebeest, especially when these are crossing streams or rivers where they are slowed down, where there is often a bit of cover for hunters, and where the prey's escape may be cut off by river banks or thickets.

There are other techniques that lions can use to get food. A few prey animals, such as a very newborn wildebeest calf, or warthog piglets, can be pursued until they are overtaken, although long distance chasing is not what lions are designed for and does not succeed with most animals. In my woodland study area in the Serengeti, lionesses when really hungry in the wet season when the soil was not rock hard, would sometimes dig for hours to remove the roof of the burrow of a warthog and seize the pig as it eventually fled. In some desert areas in southern Africa, some lions specialize on porcupines, which they manage to kill, in spite of the spines which usually protect these slow-moving animals well enough.

Some of the food that lions consume is already dead before the lion gets to it. Of course some lions in a group are in effect scavenging from the kills that their companions have made. But in addition, a lion pride may well come across the carcass of an animal that has died of natural causes, and then they will not hesitate to feed on it. Vultures and hyaenas are both more efficient and more mobile scavengers than lions are, so they will usually find such a carcass first. But the sight of vultures dropping down from the skies, or the yelps of squabbling hyaenas, will often alert a lion to the possibility of some free food, and if the lion gets there quickly its size enables it to take over whatever is left. In the magnificent Ngorongoro Crater in Tanzania, Hans Kruuk found that some lions were getting a large proportion of their food by robbing hyaenas, who in this case had caught the prey themselves. There the roles were reversed, with hyaenas doing the hunting, at night in large packs, and lions doing the scavenging afterwards.

With all this uncertainty, lions in the wild do not get a regular supply of food. Their life consists of a series of feasts, interspersed with hungry gaps of unpredictable length. If suitable prey are around, a lion pride will probably make a kill every one to three nights; all individuals should manage to fill their stomachs then, and be comfortable until the next occasion. If prey is in very

A familiar early morning scene, with a lion pride finishing
off the previous night's kill, before leaving the remains to the vultures.

A lioness pulls down a wildebeest she has managed to catch. The prey is killed usually by suffocation, with the lion's jaws clamped tightly on its throat or muzzle.

short supply for a few days, the lions seem then to switch to greater effort, travelling much further in search of food, and then usually managing to get it.

In the Serengeti, the amount of food around varies with the seasons. In the wet season, the open grass plains are full of thronging wildebeest, zebras and gazelles, and the lion prides living on or around the plains are feasting. At the same time, the woodland lion prides are struggling to survive by catching just enough of the woodland resident prey species – impala, warthog, hartebeest and buffalo. In the dry season the positions are reversed.

The plains are almost uninhabitable for lions then, and the prides at the edges of the plains are hard pressed to catch gazelles, each of which provides only a very poor meal for a group of lions. Meanwhile the woodland resident lions are finding their ranges teeming with the huge extra numbers of migratory wildebeest and zebras. For lion prides 50 miles (80 km) apart, your good or bad times depend very much on where you live.

There is strong seasonality in food abundance in many other places in Africa too. The critical thing for lions to survive there is that a habitat must have just enough suitable and catchable prey animals throughout the year in the worst of years. A lion pride cannot live in a place that is usually teeming with food if even only occasionally that place is empty.

Africa-wide, the main prey species are the commonest middle-sized ones, such as zebra and wildebeest, plus hartebeest, waterbuck and gemsbok. Lions take a number of larger species, such as eland, giraffe and buffalo, getting particularly the young or the solitary males of the last of these. Then there is a whole range of smaller animals that are occasionally preyed upon by lions, including impala, gazelles, kob, reedbuck, warthog and a host of others. There is no indication that lions have preferences from among the menu – basically they take what they can get. This is not necessarily a random sample from what is there, because some species may be more catchable than others, but there is no evidence that to a lion the taste of some prey animals is superior to that of others.

In some places, predation by lions can have a significant effect on the prey population. Locally, for example, lions are estimated to kill some 42 per cent of wildebeest in a study area in Kruger National Park in South Africa. Elsewhere, the variety and mobility of prey and the range of large predator species generally mean that lion predation alone does not have a major impact on the prey population size. Nonetheless, predation by lions and others clearly has huge indirect effects in influencing the behavior of the prey and in removing slower individuals; it probably helps reduce the spread of disease, and selects for genetically fit prey animals.

Lions are the dominant predator in Africa, being the largest and in places the most abundant. They have rivals. Leopards, living and hunting solitarily and taking a wide variety of smaller prey, are found even more widely distributed in Africa. Lions hate them, and chase them whenever they meet, but leopards find safe haven up in trees, where they can feed in peace. Cheetahs, solitary and lightly built for speed, catch their small antelope prey (mainly gazelles and impala) after a high-speed chase; they avoid lions, which find and kill a significant proportion of their cubs. Hyaenas are primarily scavengers, able even to crack and dissolve the bones of the carcasses they find. In places, spotted hyaenas are abundant enough to live in groups and sometimes hunt living prey in groups at night, and then a large pack can see off a lion. Wild dogs are scarce everywhere; they live in close-knit small packs, hunting prey by means of a very long and tiring daytime chase. All five species of predator have an impact on some of the prey species, as well as on one another. Because they hunt in different ways, their prey cannot evolve sure means of escape from any of them.

A lion wrinkles his nose ('flehmen') in response to the smell of a lioness' urine.

Social Lions

A lion pride is a family, and a very long-lasting one. Our long-term records of lion prides in the Serengeti show that the lionesses in a pride were invariably born and brought up in that pride. Strangers are never permitted to join. In consequence, the females are all related to one another, because they are the offspring of related mothers: they are mothers, daughters, grandmothers, granddaughters, aunts and cousins and so on.

The adult males in a pride are not related to the females, because they grew up somewhere else. But they are usually close relatives of one another, because in most cases they have grown up together in a pride of female relatives, and have stayed together since leaving them. By making certain reasonable assumptions about lion reproduction, I was able to calculate that in a typical Serengeti pride, the males will on average be about as closely related to one another as half-brothers, whereas the females will on average be about as closely related as first cousins. This is the family pride background in which most lion interactions take place.

For most of the time, life in a lion pride is as friendly as it is restful. The animals lie inactive in close proximity in the heat of the day, perhaps patiently sharing a small patch of annoyingly moving shade. They are tolerant of small cubs, which bump into them, or stalk them, or try to savage the tuft on the end of their tail. As they gradually, with frequent yawning, rouse themselves and their companions shortly before dusk after a hard day's resting, a great deal of sociable head-rubbing in greeting goes on, some social grooming of one another's head and neck, and brief bounding play, especially among the younger animals. In general they are more likely to direct their activities towards lions of similar age and sex as themselves, rather than randomly

Ngorongoro Crater in Tanzania provides abundant lion food all year round.

*Three young cubs follow a lioness to a daytime resting place. The smaller ones
have only recently emerged from the thickets where they were born a month or so earlier. The
larger one belongs to another lioness in the pride. They are being cared for communally.*

towards any pride members. The group moves off together, in search of water or prey, and in concert the group thunders out its roars.

I have described how lions hunt cooperatively. They do other things together too. When I came across a female in estrus in a pride, other lionesses in that same pride were also likely to be in estrus at the same time. Somehow, by still unknown means, the lionesses tend to synchronize their estrous periods with their pride companions. As a result, more than one of the males in the pride is likely to be occupied with mating. Male lions adhere to a convention that the first in possession of her has ownership rights which will not be challenged by another male. Since most matings do not result in cubs, it may be that there is rather little for the males to compete for, and indeed consortships are shared fairly evenly among the males – there is no detectable hierarchy among them.

Pride members grooming one another.

Lionesses also tend to synchronize with their pride companions when they will give birth. The mechanism by which they do so is not known at all. However, the result is that a lion pride is likely to have one or two batches of several cubs born to different mothers at around the same time as one another. After the first few weeks, all such cubs travel around together and are reared together. At one stage, one large pride in the Serengeti had a total of 24 cubs, all being reared as a batch by their eight mothers and two other lionesses. Some mothers may stay near and guard the cubs while others are away, and this synchronizing of births would appear to make cub rearing less difficult.

Adolescent male lions growing up in a pride are brothers,
half-brothers and cousins. They will form and remain a permanent team.

Synchronizing births in this way means that more than one lioness in a pride is lactating at the same time. In these circumstances, a lioness allows other cubs, not just her own, to suckle from her, almost indiscriminately at times. I have no doubt that she can recognize her own cubs, so mistaken identity is not the cause of this altruistic behavior. Very few mammals will suckle offspring that are not their own; this unusually social bit of behavior by a lioness is probably connected with the fact that the cubs being suckled are, if not her sons or daughters perhaps her grandchildren or other related animals, in whom she has a genetical interest. Cubs that are being reared communally are more likely to survive than cubs without same-age companions, and young males particularly need male companions in order to have a successful breeding life, so it is in a female's interests to help the other lionesses' cubs to survive alongside hers.

Assistant mothers are close relatives.

When the young males leave their pride at around three years old, they go as a group of young males together. If a young male has no companions when he leaves, he may team up with another solitary male in the course of his travels, or occasionally with a pair of young males. But if there are three or more in the group, no further males are accepted, so big groups of males are always all close relatives. They benefit from one another's support in being able to tackle and pull down very large prey such as bull buffaloes, in being able to push smaller groups of scavenging lions off carcasses, eventually in taking over a pride as the breeding adult males there.

Pride ownership for a male is when he is in his prime. He and his companions do not need to hunt for themselves then, and can feed on the animals that their lionesses have caught. He mates repeatedly with pride females who come into estrus, and indeed he may spend nearly 20 per cent of his time with such females. He is supported by his companions, and by the lionesses, in keeping neighboring prides where they belong. And he and his companions support one another against new groups of males trying to oust them. In the Serengeti we found that large groups of up to six males were able to keep tenure of prides for much longer than pairs could (whereas singletons rarely managed at all), and fathered many more surviving offspring.

Lions obviously do well in their social groups. The males benefit from one another's support, and from the hunting efforts of the females. All gain by group repulsion of potential intruders and scavengers. The lionesses benefit from one another's help in rearing their cubs, and in helping to provide a safety net in case a lioness should be sick or injured. They also benefit by hunting in groups. So if it is such a good arrangement, why are not all cats social, instead of only the lion? The snag of course is that every kill that a lioness makes has to be shared among a whole lot of other lions' bellies too. The social way of life is only possible if many of the potential prey are large enough to provide a good meal for several lions. Then social life becomes advantageous if the country is so open and the lion population pressure so great that a lioness' kills are otherwise likely to be witnessed and plundered and if her daughters are unlikely to be able to find anywhere else to settle; in these circumstances, they all do best if the daughters stay with their mother, as young lionesses do. For most cat species, living at lower population densities and where there are fewer medium-sized prey and where plundering is less possible, a solitary life is the only practicable choice.

Lion cubs have disproportionately large ears, and faint spots on their legs.

Cubs must wait for the adults to catch food for them.

Less Social Lions

Although they are social animals, lions often behave unsociably in pursuit of their own individual interests. Disputes can start early, and I have heard quite small, still unseen, cubs snarling at one another as they squabbled over their mother's nipples. A lioness has four nipples, and unlike with some domestic cats and a few other species there is apparently no system of individual teat ownership. A lion cub may attempt to suckle from any of its mother's nipples, trying to push away another cub that may be there first; the other responds by holding on tight, using its paws to swat or push away the newcomer. Both snarl loudly.

Squabbling over nipples gets more vigorous as the cubs get older, and as communal suckling develops. Then there may be several cubs simultaneously trying to get milk from one lioness. She clearly finds the struggle uncomfortable, will often add her snarls to the chorus, and often ends the suckling attempts by rolling over onto her front or getting up and moving off.

There is no pecking order among the cubs, such that one is consistently dominant over another. Nor is there among the remarkably egalitarian adults. No lioness is regularly displaced by another, and none has superior access to food or resting places. Over small pieces of food, small enough to be carried, there is a prior ownership convention. The animal who has the piece of food is temporarily dominant by virtue of possession of it, and others will not attack him or her. They may wait close by, and will take an opportunity to seize it if it is not closely attended, but in general ownership is respected. At large carcasses, too large to be carried away, other animals are usually permitted to join in the feeding, with perhaps a few snarls but little aggression. In normal circumstances, when food is in good supply, the system works well, and all animals in the pride get a share.

However, when there is a food shortage, and particularly if the kills are small, the situation is different. Then, strength is what counts. A larger animal will

seize the food item that a smaller has got hold of, and a fierce snarling swatting tug-of-war results. Big animals do best in these struggles, and therefore the adult males manage to get at least the lion's share of a small carcass, with the lionesses getting some, and often the cubs, being smaller and weaker, getting none. As a result, cubs can starve to death, as happened in some Serengeti prides at lean times. Prides living at the edge of the plains sometimes had only the little Thomson's gazelles available as possible prey in their territory in a bad dry season; the lions were managing to catch a few of them, but a small gazelle is quickly torn apart and devoured by the larger hungry animals. Starving cubs are not maltreated, nor treated unsociably; but during a struggling feeding frenzy at a small kill, their food is grabbed by someone else.

Later on, young males will be made to feel unwelcome in the pride. As we have seen, they all leave at around three years old, partly it seems because they are distanced, shunned and threatened by the adults, and

Play among cubs diminishes with hunger.

partly because it is becoming harder for them to get enough food from the lionesses' kills. In the course of their subsequent nomadic travels, they will have many encounters and skirmishes with other nomadic scavenging groups, and will be harried by the resident lions through whose territories they pass.

The main fighting in a lion's life comes at perhaps four to five years old when he and his companions target and try to take over a pride of lionesses

A young male, with the early stages of his mane.

and its territory. A pride is vulnerable to takeover if it has pride males who are getting on in age, or who are fewer in number than the newcomers. The resident males, sometimes assisted by the females, may chase the new males, but may not be able to drive them away completely.

Fights between males are short and dreadful. The animals rake at one another with their claws, each trying to keep his face out of range but to land a bite on his opponent with his powerful piercing canine teeth which are like strong pointed daggers. His mane protects his neck a bit, and big tufts of mane may be ripped out during a fight. Lions do not fight like gentlemen. A lion facing two opponents is in trouble, because his back is vulnerable to one enemy's teeth from behind while he is fending off the other. These fights really are about life and death. The loser may well be killed, and even if not killed his life after being ousted from a pride will be difficult and short. The winner on the other hand has ahead of him the prospect of a good reproductive life in joint possession of a pride of breeding lionesses.

Having managed at last to take over a new pride and its territory, the new males begin their reign by indulging in infanticide. They seek out and kill many or all of the small cubs there may be in the pride. They kill them quickly and easily, with a powerful bite or two, and do not usually eat the corpse, although they may do so on occasion. Cubs and their mothers will try to avoid incoming males and the fate they bring with them, but they may not manage to do so for long enough. A lioness may try to defend her cubs, but there is rather little she can do against determined infanticidal males.

The ultimate reason that males are determined to kill cubs is that they will leave more of their own descendants if they do. A lioness generally gives birth again when her first cubs are about two years old, if they survive, or about nine months after their death, if they die – as perhaps 50-75 per cent

A resting lion is nonetheless a fearsome potential fighter.

of cubs do – from disease, food shortage or violence. Therefore by killing young cubs when he takes over a pride, an incoming male can make the mother of those killed cubs give birth again sooner, to offspring that this time he and his companions will have fathered, and towards which he will be gentle and tolerant. In addition, those new cubs will not have competition from older half-siblings, which our records indicate hinder their survival chances. It all (quite unconsciously, of course) makes good biological sense to the male, and is a way in which natural selection has favored a trait because of the advantages it confers on the breeding individual, regardless of the fact that it is clearly detrimental to other individuals and to the species as a whole. It is tough on the cubs, but good for the replacements who will soon be born.

During the few years that the males are in possession of a pride, they take a share in defending the pride's territory. The male patrols it, traveling at his steady walking pace, meeting up at times with pride lionesses or male companions, perhaps sharing their kills, and driving out any intruders he may encounter. Territory boundaries are not precise, and lions do not fight over what are the exact limits of their territory. All concerned seem to know roughly where they are at home and where they are in someone else's home, and appear to be less confident when they are near the edges of their range. An intruder is chased out, but often gently, it seems. It looks very much as though the owner does not actually want to catch the intruder, and indeed both animals generally slow to a steady walking pace. It probably makes more sense to escort an intruder out, rather than to catch and have to fight with him or her.

Lions let others know, both by sound and by smell, that their territory is occupied. The lion's roar is a magnificent sound: a few deep impressive moans fading off into a series of gruff grunts, but with the power and resonance to thrill any nearby hearer on a quiet African night. Very often a whole group

A large dark mane makes its owner look larger and more daunting.

roars at the same time, not in strict unison but with the different animals' calls roared out independently as part of the chorus. The sound travels for a mile or two, and very often back will come a rumbling answering chorus from another group, perhaps other members of the same pride or perhaps the neighbors also asserting their claim in turn. Roaring makes clear not only which individuals are where, but also that they consider that they belong there, and intruders will often depart abruptly on hearing the owners' roars. All the large cats of the genus *Panthera* can roar, as a result of having cartilage in place of the hyoid bone at the base of the skull, but none of the others can match the lion's roar for loudness or grandeur.

A roar is gone as soon as it stops being made. Scent can last far longer. Males scent-mark their territory at intervals as they travel. A male approaches a bush, sniffs at the leaves, briefly rubs his head through them, then brings his rear end to them and with his tail held high he squirts powerful sprays of urine, with anal gland secretions, onto the vegetation. As a result he has left a message on his olfactory noticeboard, saying who was there and when. At other times he will squirt the urine onto his hind feet as he scrapes them on the ground, and so leaves scented footprints wherever he goes. No intruding lion is in any doubt that a lion territory is occupied.

Maintaining territories involves a considerable amount of work, because they can be quite large. In good lion habitat, such as the Serengeti, with prey available all year round, a small pride might occupy as little as 10 sq miles (25 sq km), and a large pride perhaps four times as much. In places, lions may use ranges that are far larger than that — as vast as 770 sq miles (2000 sq km) in Etosha — as prey availability changes in different parts of the area; but they will not be trying to defend the whole of such a large area at the same time, and big ranges like that will usually overlap a great deal.

A lion's mane helps to protect his neck during fights.

Lions and Humans

Some of our forebears in Ice Age Europe were familiar enough with lions to scratch into the walls of caves in France superb depictions of the great cave lions that lived in the area ten or twenty thousand years ago. From very early times, lions have been venerated, as illustrated in ancient Egyptian paintings and sculptures, and manifested in the Ancient Egyptian cities of Leontopolis and Heliopolis where priests looked after live lions as though they were gods.

The writings of Aristotle and Pliny, for centuries unquestioned as reliable sources, related numerous accounts of lions, of their chivalry towards women, of the miscegenation by lionesses with hyaenas to produce monsters, and on occasion of their unexpected meekness and gentleness, giving rise to the story of Androcles and many others. The lion receives 130 mentions in the Bible, often metaphorically, such as 'the righteous are bold as a lion', on which basis many rulers have been given leonine labels: Richard the Lionhearted, Henry the Lion and many others through history. The 'King of the Beasts' tag had been acquired by the lion by the first century AD. Lions have featured widely in art for the past three thousand years, in Bushman art, in Saharan rock drawings, on pottery and furniture from Egyptian tombs, on buildings throughout the Middle East and India, and of course in pictures and sculptures throughout the West. Lions have played a large part in heraldry and all its spin-offs, from nicknames to pub signs, as well as in mythology and astrology.

People have made practical use of lions too, in all manner of ways. A maned lion headdress is worn as a sign of valor among men of African tribes such as the Masai and Samburu, and indeed in being awarded to the man who first seized the hunted lion's tail is no empty symbol when you are hunting with spears. Lion fat is said to be good for treating carbuncles, ear-ache and

Concealment from human beings is often a lion's best strategy.

rheumatic pains; wearing or carrying lions' teeth, claws or whiskers protects the wearer against enemies; eating a lion's eyes will improve your eyesight; and eating a lion's heart will give you courage: these and other notions underlie the occasional use of lion parts, but in general the demand is limited and local.

Live lions have been extensively exploited, especially as fighters. Rameses II, Pharaoh of Egypt, was accompanied into battle by a lion who ran alongside his chariot. Lions were set to fight against one another, against other species, and against human warriors in the increasingly spectacular and bloody circuses of Ancient Rome. Influential status-conscious Romans sometimes kept tamed lions, for pulling them around in a chariot.

Hunting lions has been a popular minority pursuit down the ages. In times past it was often necessary for protecting livestock against predation by lions, but it was also clearly a significant sport in itself. Numerous African tribes have lion-hunting traditions, going back generations. In around 1400 BC, the Pharaoh Amenhotep III hunted hundreds of lions, shooting them with bow and arrow from his war chariot. Others, including Saint Louis, the Moghul emperors, and the Tuareg people of the Niger region, hunted lions from horseback, using arrows, lances and spears. British sportsmen in India, and Dutch settlers in southern

Many parts of a lion are valued as folklore medicines.

A lion out in the open is relatively easily hunted.

48

Africa shot them from horseback or on foot. Nowadays, big game sport or trophy hunters can be transported in comfortable vehicles to the general vicinity of a lion. The accompanying 'white hunter' locates the lion, perhaps by baiting beforehand, guides the client for the relatively small amount of footwork, tells him when to shoot, protects him against attack, provides backup shots if the client's are insufficient, and photographs him in triumph with his trophy.

Sometimes the killing is the other way round, and lions take to man-eating. What is surprising really is how rare this is, given the vulnerability of human beings compared with lions' normal prey species. Nonetheless, lions which take to preying on people almost always end up being killed by determined hunting parties of human beings. Man-eaters do not know this, of course, but a sensible fear of human beings is quite deeply ingrained in wild lions. It is not clear what induces the occasional lion to take its first human being: sometimes perhaps extreme hunger as a result of injury or prey shortage, or having scavenged from a human corpse beforehand, or an exceptionally easy opportunity, or perhaps the example of a companion lion. Once started on man-eating the lion tends to continue to prey on people, and becomes cunning and bold in doing so. The two famous 'Man-eaters of Tsavo' devoured dozens of laborers working on building the Uganda Railway at the end of the nineteenth century, seriously delayed the construction work, and spread terror in the vicinity. 'Chiengi Charlie', as a large pale lion was called, had a similar reign of terror a decade later in what is now north-west Zambia, and there are many other examples. They make good reading a century later when you are far from the deadly reality of the events.

More of lions' attention is generally devoted to people's livestock than to the people themselves. Cattle constitute very easy prey for lions, being slow,

Large canine teeth equip lions for killing prey, including the human species.

abundant, defenceless, and apparently stupid. It is not too difficult for a lion to ambush a grazing herd of cattle, but if it does it will bring down on itself the attention of the herdsman and his friends. Very often, grazing cattle are attended by small boys, who can alert villagers to any lion presence or attack. The herdsboys are not particularly at risk themselves, for it is difficult to imagine a lion selecting for its meal a scrawny boy in preference to a substantial cow or bullock. Cattle are particularly vulnerable in the dark, and in lion country they all have to be brought back to safer quarters at night.

In the second half of the twentieth century, tourism has taken over from sport hunting as the main way in which people come into close contact with lions. Many thousands of tourists, mostly from Europe and North America, visit the wild areas of East and southern Africa in order to look at the wildlife and its habitat, and to experience nature still relatively unspoilt by mankind. There is no doubt that lions are one of the greatest draws. There will not be many tourist vehicles stopping to watch a group of giraffes or gazelles, for example, but they will certainly stop and admire and probably photograph a pride of lions, however inactive at the time. And because of their popularity, and hence the attention they receive from these noisy but essentially harmless vehicles, lions in many national parks in Africa have become so familiar with vehicles that they almost ignore them, enabling tourists to look at lions from very close range and appreciate them all the more.

This recently acquired tolerance by lions is not a loss of their natural fear of human beings; rather it is an acceptance that human beings in vehicles in national parks are harmless. I am sure that a lion in the Serengeti looking at a tourist minibus parked beside it knows perfectly well that those creatures moving about inside it are people. Equally, if the lion were to encounter those same people on foot he would stay clear of them. Intelligent animals such as lions learn the contexts in which they need to fear danger.

One of the benefits of wild lions' acceptance of vehicles has been that

In protected areas, lions learn that vehicles (with human beings
visible inside them) are generally harmless. Roads provide convenient routes,
free of thorns, for lions to travel along as they patrol their territory.

detailed scientific research has been made far more practicable. If you are close up to a lion, it is far easier to recognize which individual it is than if you are far away. In the Serengeti the lion scientists have established an identity card system for each lion in the main study areas, with close-up photographs, a general description, and an indication of particular distinguishing features of each lion, such as nicks in the ears, scars on the nose, and broken or missing teeth. When you know the individual, you then record systematically

when it is encountered, and where, who it is with, and what it is doing, and so over the years you build up some valuable long-term histories. It was from such records that we discovered, the beneficial effects for lionesses of synchronising births with their companions, and the extent of infanticide by incoming males, and the value to pride males of having companions.

Early morning is the best time to find lions.

In the Serengeti, research has been able to go considerably further too, thanks to an enlightened attitude by the National Park managers. Being permitted to immobilize lions by darting them allowed the use of radio-tracking, which I pioneered with lions in East Africa. Being able to find known lions consistently meant that it was at last possible to find out just where they went in the difficult woodland areas of the Serengeti, what size ranges they needed, what they fed on there at different seasons, and how they depended on and influenced the prey species there.

With experience, you find that every lion looks different, provided you are close enough.

Similarly useful information has since been gathered by radio-tracking studies elsewhere too.

In the past decade, molecular genetical studies have also produced an enormous amount of information. They have been based on the blood (and sometimes semen) samples that it has been possible to take from darted and so immobilized (but otherwise completely unharmed) lions of known life histories in the Serengeti region. These studies have confirmed, for example, that male and female lions are indeed closely related to the same-sex members of their pride but not to their mating partners, and that the same male is the father of all the cubs in a litter, even if a lioness mated with more than one male. The studies have also revealed that some males in coalitions apparently father many fewer cubs than others, for still unknown reasons. At the population level, these studies have shown that the lions in the nearby Ngorongoro Crater are derived from the Serengeti population but as a result of a drastic fall in numbers 40 years ago and some inbreeding since, the Ngorongoro lions show less genetic diversity and more sperm abnormalities. They may be in trouble in the future.

Comparing genetic samples taken from lions in East and South Africa has also shown that they are all pretty similar. There really does not seem to be justification for keeping the names (*senegalensis*, *somaliensis*, *massaicus*, *krugeri*, *roosevelti*, *bleyenberghi*, and so on) of the various subspecies of *Panthera leo* that were described from different parts of Africa in the nineteenth century and the first third of the twentieth. The descriptions are mostly based on one or two skins and skulls that may not have been in any way representative of the local lion population as a whole. We now know, from close observation of living animals, how much natural variation there is among the individual animals even within one small study area.

Lions spend most of their lives resting.

The Future for Lions

If our hundred-greats grandparents had been able to produce a lion distribution map, it would have shown that lions were quite a widely spread species then, much more than they are now 3000 years later. At that time, as well as being found almost throughout Africa, they were also distributed from Greece to north-eastern India, in a strip that included Turkey, Israel, Syria, parts of Arabia, Iraq, Iran, Afghanistan and Pakistan. Even at that stage, the lion's range was already declining, and the process has accelerated since. Within the past 200 years, they have disappeared in Africa from the southern tip and from north of the Sahara, and virtually throughout their vast Asian range.

The trend is clear. Absolute numbers are unknown, but the world's lion population at the present time is estimated at somewhere between 30,000 and 100,000 animals. They are most widespread and abundant in Kenya, Tanzania, Ethiopia, Central African Republic, Zaire, Zambia, and Botswana. Elsewhere, lions are sparse, and largely restricted to protected areas.

The reason for the decline is also clear: the human species, in increasing numbers, whose interests conflict with those of lions. In many parts of the lion's range, large areas have been appropriated by mankind for cultivation or human habitation. When that happens, there is clearly no place either for lions or for the wild prey on which they depend, and the species rapidly disappears. In many places, where the pressure on land may not be as strong yet, the domestic livestock that human beings look after indirectly causes a decline in lion numbers. It happens for two reasons. First, the livestock competes with the wild prey species for the limited amount of grazing available; with their human protectors and with access to the water that human beings provide for their stock, the cattle, sheep and goats have an unfair advantage over the

Lions have disappeared from much of their range; their numbers are declining fast.

wild grazing animals, and their numbers rise, often at the cost of degradation of the habitat. As a result there is less wild lion food around. Second, partly because of this, lions will prey on livestock, understandably the owners of such livestock take strong measures to protect their future livelihood. Lions that prey on cattle are quickly shot, or poisoned using easily available agricultural pesticides in baited carcasses. They are not that difficult to eradicate, if people want to do so, and it is understandable that in many cases, sadly, some people do want to exterminate what they see as a threat to their living.

Increasingly in the future, lions will be tolerated only in protected areas such as national parks and game reserves. The hope has to be that these protected areas themselves will be preserved and maintained in the long term, and that lions (and other animals) will be safe inside them. In principle, such areas can bring significant amounts of money into the African country from overseas, either from tourism or from trophy hunting.

A lioness carries her young cub to a new hiding place.

In practice it is not quite as straightforward. For a start, the two approaches are mutually incompatible in the same area. Tourists individually spend rather little locally — much of their money goes on air fares, petrol, and imported drink, food or film — so you need large numbers of tourists, as well as unafraid animals for them to look at. But the trophy-hunter values, and pays a great deal for, the reverse: an environment where he is almost on his own, pitted against elusive and possibly

*Play helps to prepare lion cubs for their adult world.
They learn by practising how to stalk, pounce, wrestle and fight. They
also learn when to give way to a more powerful adversary.*

*Predation by lions helps to keep prey populations fit and alert,
but does not usually have a long term effect on the size of those populations.*

dangerous animals. It is not easy for a country to advertize one of these types of experience very vigorously without damaging the image of the other one.

Fashions in overseas visiting are liable to be fickle, and disease or civil unrest in one African country can irrationally deter foreign visits to the whole continent. Thus it is by no means certain that protected areas will necessarily be able to pay their way by attracting foreigners to them in the future. In many cases, with the development of more efficient crops, such as low-rainfall maize, some areas which used to be unsuitable for cultivation can now produce crops commercially, and potentially could bring greater financial benefit to the country than from wildlife and foreign visitors. Governments may be tempted, or pressured by a land-hungry population, to allow the land to be ploughed up.

An emaciated lion, feeding on morsels.

Maintaining protected areas for wildlife ultimately depends on the support of the local people living nearby. They rarely get much financial benefit themselves from the wildlife, yet they are the ones who face most of the overspill problems: it is their crops that are nibbled by antelopes or flattened by elephants, or their livestock that are plundered by lions or leopards. There will always be edge problems around reserves, unless these are fenced off with formidably expensive game fences. Some young lions expelled from their successful prides protected inside reserves are likely to wander outside and come into fatal contact with livestock. There is little option but to destroy such animals quickly and compensate the farmers, who may otherwise take reprisals. But compensation schemes have all sorts of drawbacks.

Shrinking of their habitat is the biggest long-term threat to lion populations in Africa, but there are others too. Disease can strike down healthy lions. In the early 1990s, there was an outbreak of canine distemper in lions in the Serengeti region, which wiped out about a third of the roughly 3000 lions there. The virus came from domestic dogs living with the pastoral Masai people around the edges of the park, and thanks to speedy investigation a dog vaccination programme has now been set up there to try to prevent a recurrence of the problem. Infection across species is worrying.

As the lion population becomes fragmented into reserves, some of the small subpopulations may well be so small that inbreeding among related animals starts to happen; if it does, some of the genetic diversity of the animals will disappear, the sub-population will become less resistant to disease, and fertility could start to decline. We saw early indications of such changes in Ngorongoro. Vigorous management, involving transferring lions (as live animals, or as sperm or embryos) between reserves may become necessary in some places, in order to overcome these small-population effects.

Threats to wildlife are liable to change rapidly. A fairly recent threat that is decimating the wild tiger population at the moment is the suddenly more widespread demand for tiger parts (bones, claws, penis) for charms, tonics and potions in the growingly affluent human populations in South East Asia, especially China, South Korea and Taiwan. I am not confident, even with the great efforts of conservationists and others, that wild tiger populations will be able to survive this onslaught: there may be no wild tigers left in a couple of decades, so lucrative is the trade in tiger parts. Lions play no part in oriental medicine, fortunately, but virtually nobody can distinguish a lion bone from a tiger bone, so they could easily be substituted. Poaching lions would be far less difficult than poaching tigers, and with a price on their bodies lions could be badly hit by a sudden onset of illegal hunting. I hope it will never happen, but would not feel too sure that it won't.

Worldwide, populations of large carnivores such as this Gir Forest lion do not combine well with the farming activities of ever more numerous human beings.

Although the African lion is still widespread, the Asiatic lion hangs on only by a whisker or two. Its only wild population anywhere in the world is in the Gir Forest in north-west India, where there are about 250-300 of them, as many as their sanctuary can hold. Asiatic lions (*Panthera leo persica*) differ little from African ones: they tend to have small manes, always have a fold of skin running lengthways along the underside of the belly (African lions rarely do), and often have the infraorbital foramen (a small hole in a skull bone) divided into two rather than single as always in African lions. Their general behavior is pretty much the same as that of their African close relatives.

The Gir Forest lions survived there because it was the private hunting ground of the Nawab of Junagadh, and the lion population there was below 100 at the beginning of the twentieth century. The area contains a large human population, the Maldharis, and their 14,000 livestock, in the wildlife sanctuary surrounding the small core national park. The numbers of wild prey (particularly axis and sambar deer) have increased greatly in the past two decades since some of the Maldharis were moved out of the park. Even so, perhaps a third of the lions' food is livestock, and their owners are becoming less tolerant, despite government compensation, of the lions' predation on their stock. Also whereas the lions have in the past been relatively docile towards their human neighbors, in recent years they have become more aggressive towards them, and there have been many more lion attacks on people. There is a risk that the Maldharis will retaliate. Meanwhile human activities in the area are damaging the environment, by fires, encroachment, disturbance, pollution and the taking out of firewood. The situation is a foretaste of the same problems that may be played out in many reserves in Africa in years to come.

There are a number of Asiatic lions in captivity. The responsible zoos of

Yawning is contagious, among lions as among human beings.

the world manage co-ordinated captive breeding programs for threatened species such as the Asiatic lion. A few years ago, many of the captive population of this subspecies were shown by molecular genetic research to contain some African lion blood, as a result of some undocumented mixing of the subspecies long ago. The program is now being rebuilt, using known pure animals, of which there is a surplus from the thriving Gir population. There are plans to establish back-up wild populations in one or two other areas in India, as a safety net against disease or other disaster.

Lions breed easily in captivity; indeed they were being bred by the Assyrian kings as early as 860 BC. Nowadays, in major zoos the vast majority of captive lions, almost all of them African, are not being bred because the zoos of the world are as full of lions as they want to be, and it would be very difficult to find homes for lion cubs. Most zoo lionesses are on contraception, by means of a small hormone implant injected below the skin which prevents ovulation for a couple of years.

They may do very well in zoos, but lions belong in the wild. They can be put back there, with difficulty, as George and Joy Adamson first showed with the lioness Elsa in *Born Free*. Reintroduction of lions into the wild only makes sense if suitable habitat is available. But if it is, why is it not fully occupied by lions already? Do the factors that resulted in the absence of lions there no longer apply? And if you are introducing lions into a patch of wilderness in Africa, it will generally be less difficult to do using already wild-living lions from elsewhere. That way they will already have the skills they will need: to conserve their energy and effort through the scorching days and crisp nights; to stalk, ghostlike, the nimble antelopes they will seize, strangle and devour; to suckle and rear the squawking furry cubs they will produce; to remain within the huge hot territory they will occupy; and to steer clear of us noisy, overabundant human beings.

A King of the Beasts, in his prime in his pride.

Present-day Distribution of Lions in Africa

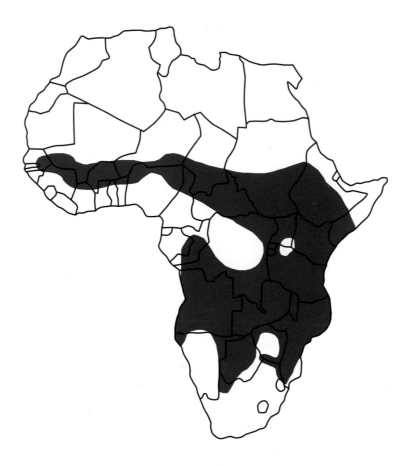

In most countries within the species' range, lions are nowadays mainly to be found within protected areas. A map drawn a couple of centuries earlier would have shown lions over almost the whole continent except for the rainforest and driest deserts.

Map redrawn from *Wild Cats*: Nowell & Jackson (eds), International Union for Conservation of Nature and Natural Resources, Gland, 1996.

Lion Facts

Scientific Name	*Panthera leo*
Common Names	English: Lion
	Swahili: Simba
Ave. Adult Weight	Male: 399 lbs (181 kg)
	Female: 276 lbs (125 kg)
Total Length (inc. tail)	Male: 148 in (3.75 m)
	Female: 132 in (3.35 m)
Shoulder Height	37 in (94 cm)
Gestation Period (Days)	110 (range 100–114)
Litter Size	usually 2–4 (range 1–6)
Longevity (Years)	12–20 (longer in captivity)
Daily Food Requirements	11–15 lbs (5–7 kg)

Recommended Reading

C.A.W. Guggisberg's book *Simba, the Life of the Lion* (Howard Timmins, Cape Town, 1961) is a gold mine of historical information about lions. *The Serengeti Lion* by George Schaller (University of Chicago Press, 1972) gives a wealth of data, particularly on predation, from the first scientific study of lions in the wild. Most data since have been published in scientific papers, later summarized and condensed in books. *Pride of Lions* (J.M. Dent, London, 1978) by Brian Bertram concentrates particularly on lion social organization and its evolution. Craig Packer's *Into Africa* (University of Chicago Press, 1994) brings the subject much more up to date, outlining another two decades of research, its trials and tribulations as well as its results. To put lions into context, *Great Cats*, edited by John Seidensticker and Susan Lumpkin (Rodale Press, Emmaus, 1991) provides a fine introduction to the large cats. The latest conservation information on wild cats, large and small, has been assembled by Kristin Nowell and Peter Jackson, editors of *Wild Cats* (International Union for Conservation of Nature and Natural Resources, Gland, 1996); it consists of a status survey and conservation action plan, produced by IUCN/SSC Cat Specialist Group members, for all of the world's species of wild cats.

Index

*Entries in **bold** indicate pictures*

Biographical Note

Brian Bertram has been involved with a wide variety of animals. Fresh from a Ph.D. from Cambridge University on mynah birds in India, he studied lions (and leopards and others) in the Serengeti National Park in Tanzania, and established the long-term study programme for lions there. He worked on ostrich breeding behavior in Kenya while a Senior Research Fellow at King's College in Cambridge. He was Curator of Mammals (and also of the Aquarium and Invertebrates) at London Zoo, and then Director General of The Wildfowl & Wetlands Trust at Slimbridge. He is now a freelance Zoological Adviser.